unbroken

julie skon

ISBN 979-8-9852794-0-5

dear jovani,

you showed me that
love is what heals the parts of us that feel broken

i am forever grateful for you

love,
jules

dear daughters,

life is a journey
of experiences
that teach you how to love
deeper

but nothing has taught me
more about love
than you

mama

i am broken

cracked wide open
split in two
torn
between a laugh at a memory
and the ache of missing it

the first time i saw him
the earth stood still
his name was jovani
i can't write about him
without telling you his name

with him
i felt everything
an ache in my body next to him
his warm breath upon my skin
the energy of what was not needed to be said

his heart so big
it would make your soul cry
every moment
with him
i felt alive

there was a second time the earth stood still

when the woman in the white coat spoke
she said jovani was broken
a bullet broke him
cracked his heart wide open
tore him from a place where i could breathe and he could not

broken
both of us
broken

———

she said
i had to meet you
see your sparkling green eyes

i laughed and played along
the music in the background
was too loud to ask why

but when our eyes met
and the seconds slowed
something inside of me changed

i had a new feeling arise
it was intoxicatingly alive
as i thought, just maybe
you were meant to be mine

i was afraid for you to see the parts of me that hurt
but more afraid for you not to

we sat on a cement staircase
underneath scattered stars
we shared secrets
that were scars
and somehow
so quickly
my heart
became yours

he had a slanted smile
a swag with grace
always up to something
a plan hidden
in that beautiful face

rugby boots
tempura shrimp
wet kisses
skinny dips
salty air
sandy toes

we laughed
we cried
until the sun went down

when we woke

arms and legs entangled

the sun rose

and the magic began

all over again

with our heads on one pillow
we would talk

unkindness
injustice
abuse

in a soft and sad tone

the kind that makes you listen

and fall in love

again
again
and again

he would say

go ahead
let your hair down
run like a wild child into the sun

when you come back
i'll be here
waiting for you and i will declare

how you make me weak
your real self turns me on
that shy side makes me strong

and it is with you
my love
that my soul belongs

i would close my eyes
pretend to sleep

waiting for him to whisper
in his carnal way

i love you

they were the most beautiful words
i had ever heard

raw and real
hauntingly honest

it was there, in those moments
i felt i belonged

BOOM.

from air in your lungs
to flat
no heartbeat
just like that

your energy
your love
your body alone
just like that

your voice
your laugh
your touch gone
just like that

i can't breathe
i can't move
i can't think
just like that

our hearts
our dreams
our life gone
just like that

just like that
as you took your last breath
my love
my soul broke

i am

lying in the street
staring at the stars
fighting
to just have scars

did you ever see
how connected they are
the stars
our scars

baby i am bleeding
our friends are on top of me
fighting for me
to just have scars

i am fading
life is slipping
hold me in your heart
and remember...

i will always be
in the scars
and
the stars

i promise you

i will be
your forever
loving
hovering ghost

in an instant
i was forced
to try and let go
of everything
i wasn't ready
to lose

you are my sunshine
wrapped in a blanket of grief

my heart breaks
when i open my eyes
morning brings a stinging truth
i fell asleep to convincing myself it was a lie

my lungs sting
there is not enough air
breathing seems unfair
i am drowning in despair

my legs hurt
from circles of walking
i am doing a dance
around the truth i am not talking

my mind is scattered
i can't keep up with this pace
tired of finding a reason
to stay in this race

my body is shattered
pieces nowhere to be found
i am living a nightmare
my soul feels tethered and bound

they tell me tomorrow will come
and again i will roam
this heart wrenching journey
of trying to find my way home

today felt too bright
all i wanted to do was close my eyes
and be held by you

i watched you
dance
as you wept
when you slept

when you woke
i cried
as i watched
you try

to fall in love
with life
all over again

there is not a feeling as lonely
as a breath
without your love
unable to breathe next to you

i stare at the stars
feel the scars
and i think
it is possible
i am dying inside

i sat across a wooden table
from our friend today

he told me stories about his angels
you were one of them

he told me that you are tethered and bound
by love

he said that if i was strong enough
brave enough
loved enough
that i had to let you go

he said that you would
stay
you would wait
you would be destined by fate
to fight with me

until i was brave enough
to set you free

there isn't a vision
more painfully profound
than seeing your
angels
wings bound

he came to me
in my dream

he told me to
keep running like a wild child
into the wind

to find the place where the moon is rising
and the earth begins

and when i got there
to let it all go
to fall

he said he would be there to catch me
to guide my broken heart home

have you ever loved
anyone enough
to say goodbye

i just broke
on a mountain top
when i said the words goodbye

i didn't have your body to fall into
or anyone to call
to understand why

because you are mine
i am yours
i can't stand to hurt us anymore

you didn't lie on that pavement
staring at the stars
fighting to just have scars

for me to fall weak
or not be brave enough
to let you fly

and i did not
endure this heartache
to not be grounded in this skin

because there are battles to be fought
and lives to be taught
how to love

Jovani Nero Tovar, my love, our love,
our best friend, our son, our brother, our
colleague, our student, our soulmate,
was shot and killed when he was 22 years
old in a senseless act of gun violence.

He died a hero, vibrantly and
beautifully full of love for life.

A NOTE FROM THE AUTHOR

Hi, my name is Julie Skon. I wrote this poetry about Jovani Tovar, a young man that I loved who tragically lost his life to gun violence. These poems were written over many nights and years of grieving near a fireplace with a pencil and paper to turn to for healing. I never planned to release them until something inside of me told me it was time.

I am publishing unbroken on the 20 year anniversary of Jovani's passing because he taught me the beauty in vulnerability, he taught me to love wildly and deeply, and he taught me to be fearless in chasing my dreams because life is short.

Thank you for reading unbroken. I hope it touched your heart in a way that it was meant to. If you would like to say hello, share your story, have questions, or need some support, I am here for you: julie@myrituelle.com

Love, Jules